Go
Clari...
read the pages of this
book !!!
Dalene

Divorced

"Suddenly Single"

Mom's

Devotional

30 Days of Encouragement
That Addresses Your Unique Journey

Darlene Higgs Hollis

DH Books International

Divorced « Suddenly Single » Mom's Devotional
Copyright © 2017 by Darlene Higgs Hollis

Unless otherwise indicated, Scripture quotations are taken from the
New International Version of the Bible.

For information contact :
DH Books International
289 Jonesboro Road
Suite 145
McDonough, GA 30253
http://www.thecprlifecoach.com

Cover design by Angelina Jake

ISBN: 978-1981154630

First Edition: October 2017

10 9 8 7 6 5 4 3 2 1

Dedication

I dedicate this book to the memory of my friend, big sister, advisor, and Godmother to my 3 children, Gaye Hayles-Newton. This is for the book we spoke all this summer of you writing. But you made your transition before you could put the pen to paper. Your example to me and my children we now strive to emulate. Your life of prayer, faith, love and being a woman of your word. We'll love you forever. Will never forget you.

Acknowledgements

I want to thank my Heavenly Father for downloading this book through me. Without hearing from God, this book would not exist.

I would like to thank my 3 children Terykah, Trey and Tierra for being my inspiration to push forward. They are my legacy. To my 3Ts, thank you so much for believing in mommy. Thank you for always praying and encouraging me when I got tired as I was writing this book. I wish you'll would tell me who positioned the lamp to shine directly in my face so I'd wake up to stay on my writing schedule (smile).

To my friend and prayer partner Deborah Jordan, thank you so much for being there with me through most of the divorce journey I speak of in this Devotional. Thank you for standing in the gap for me to keep my sanity during those long sleepless nights.

Life Coaches Monique Caradine and Keanna Jones, thank you for waking up my dreams in a big way to remind me that I can do this; that I am destined for overflow.

Tierra Destiny Reid, thank you for reminding me that it's okay to 'pause and propel'.

To Kandace Dye, thank you so much for your support during the writing of this first book. My accountability partner Angela McGowan, you rock!! Thank you for being there whenever I needed you.

To my family, friends, ministry family and social media family, thank you for believing in me and supporting.

CONTENTS

Foreward

By Ronisa Glass

WOW!! That's truly the first "thought" I had while reading this book. It wasn't so much for the trauma, the unfortunate circumstances, nor, the at times, heartbreaking experiences. It was because I, like many other women across the world, could find ourselves intricately placed somewhere within its pages.

Darlene has managed to somehow, someway, show us the fragility of divorce and the *impact* it can make in a woman/mother's life, but she has shown us how to "Rise" from it when the dust settles and how to sweep it out of your door so that you, your children and your life, can become free from the cloud of it, clearer than ever and eventually, made whole again.

This amazing book was not only inspiring; you will read it and be encouraged. You will read it and find a new level of faith building within as well as a new fight. You *will* read it and know that like this writer, mother, sister and friend, you too can make it out! You will survive!

So, go ahead and read it. Let the words marinate in your heart and mind. You may find different emotions within these pages, but I can almost guarantee you, that you'll find a little more strength in your own personal walk.

I am so grateful for you releasing this book. Not only was it a timely writing, it's one that speaks to a different type of woman from the norm. Darlene, you *really* are, Your Sister's Keeper!

Introduction

"Lord! Does anyone really understand what I am going through? They say they do, but they don't!" This was my cry many days as I navigated this new water I was in; a single mom for the first time. Now divorced with 3 children, ages two, six and ten. It was like learning to ride a bike again. New waters that I was treading in. My head about to go under, even as I tried to hold all three children up above the water themselves.

What kept me through this period was my faith in my Lord. God would always show up just when I was ready to give up and in ways where I knew that was God speaking to me personally.

I wrote this devotional to show you that you are not alone on this journey. God has not forgotten you and your children. I pray that in the pages of this book lie words of hope for you to strengthen you as you are restored and as you rebuild yourself from the inside out; rebuild your life and the lives of your children.

Even as you try to keep all the balls in the air on this journey of being a "Suddenly Single" mom, take a few minutes each day to meditate on God's love for you.

Mind

Day 1

Kicking Fear!

Scripture: For God hath not given us the spirit of fear, but of power, and of love, and of a sound mind. 2 Timothy 1:7 (KJV)

FEAR PARALYZES! THAT IS CHRONIC FEAR. - It slows down your physical health, your memory your brain activity and your mental health. When fear is present, you can't think straight because you perceive a threat and anxiety is present. Your body gets in the fight-or-flight mode after signals are sent to the brain that danger is present. If you continue in this mode it takes its toll on the way you think. This affects the way you make decisions and the speed at which you get things done.

One of my fears after my separation and divorce was living on my own again after twelve years of having a man in the house. Now I was solely responsible for our safety. I was terrified! "What would I do if someone were to break in the house?" was at the forefront of my mind. I was afraid of taking care of myself and three children financially. In the beginning I hardly slept at night. But had to get up early to go to work.

My turning point came when my house alarm went off in the middle of the night. I was terrified! Thankfully nobody entered my home. But after this incident I made up my mind that I could not live with this paralyzing fear any longer. I had to either trust the God that I believed in to protect and take care of me and my children.

When fear comes in you cannot allow it to take over. Leave fear in its 'fight-or-flight' moment when needed. But do not carry it with you always. I began to mediate on scriptures concerning fear.

Remember that God is always with you. Turn your fear over to him.

PRAYER FOR THE DAY: *Father, I bring to you today all my fears. Please take them and help me to totally trust that you have me and my children and all that is important to us. Free my mind that I can make right decisions. Give me courage from this day forward. Amen.*

Recommended Scriptures: *Psalm 56:3; John 14:27; Philippians 4:6-7; Isaiah 41:10; Psalm 94:19*

Reflections for Today

Day 2

Conquering Pride

Scripture: When pride comes, then comes disgrace, but with humility comes wisdom   Proverbs 11:2 (NIV)

PRIDE COMETH BEFORE THE FALL. It's a statement that most of us have heard all of our lives. But why is not having so much pride important? Why do most of us divorced moms have so much of it? For most of us, pride is taught from the time we were born. Especially us females – pride is almost synonymous with beauty. More important in some cultures than others. As divorced "suddenly single" moms, we are used to not having to go outside the home to ask for anything or letting anyone know that everything is not alright, or that we need help. We want that ex-husband and everyone else to think that all is well. That outside of the ex-husband providing for his children we don't need anyone for anything else.

In looking at today's scripture reference, I'm reminded of many instances where pride caused bad things to happen or almost happen to me and my children. On several occasions, I knew I needed help, but I was determined to do it alone; try to figure it out myself. On several occasions we had no food in the house, no heat, or no electricity. And yes, I worked a fulltime great paying (most thought so) job at a university. But it was still not enough.

Once my sister, who lived in another state found out that we had no food to eat. I could not work any more miracles. Unknown to me, she called my brother who lived fifteen minutes away from me. I was so embarrassed! I didn't want anyone knowing that I was struggling, was my first thought. However, he fussed at me and said don't ever do that again. That's what family is for.

This incident was a reminder that my pride also caused my children to suffer. It was not just consequences for me. I had to put pride way, be humble and use wisdom to get what we needed.

There are times we need to speak up instead of staying silent. Don't let pride keep you in bondage.

PRAYER FOR THE DAY: *Dear Lord, having pride in the wrong place at times is a challenge for me. Please help me to be humble so that I can make wise decisions for me and my children. Help me to find ways to balance pride and humility from this day forward. Amen.*

Recommended Scriptures: *Proverbs 16:18; Psalm 73:6; Proverbs 29:23; Proverbs 14:13; Ecclesiastes 7:8*

Reflections for Today

_____

_____

_____

_____

_____

_____

_____

_____

_____

_____

_____

_____

_____

_____

_____

_____

_____

_____

_____

_____

_____

_____

_____

Day 3

Forget the Past: All Things New

Scripture: Forget the former things; do not dwell on the past.   Isaiah 43:18 (NIV)

FORGET THE FORMER THINGS; do not dwell on the past! These are easy words to say but a hard action to carry out. What! Forget the pain, forget the anger? Forget the humiliation? Forget the good memories? Forget the love? Forget the family times? It is not easy to not dwell on the past. Not easy to forget everything that happened before you got married, while you were married and even right after everything that's happened to this point. Sometimes the hurt and the pain still feels like the present.

For me, it was hard to move on when I thought about the verbal and physical abuse I endured for many years during my marriage. Many days I thought about how many years of my life I had dedicated to this relationship; eighteen years to be exact. Many Friday and Saturday nights, I sat all alone, trying to pick up the pieces of what was now my life. I felt stuck.

But, I had to draw on my faith. I had to believe that God had better for me in my future and the future of my children. Like today's scripture says, forget the former things, do not dwell on the past. The other part of that says, "see I am doing a new thing now it springs up do you not perceive it?" I had to see the new things that God was doing in my life. I began to look for the good. I began to use the past as a springboard into my future. It became experiences to make myself better, to make my children better, and to help other women who would come behind me going through the same experience.

Today, begin to use the past as fuel to move forward. Let it be a catalyst for you reaching for all those dreams you had placed on that back burner while you'd focused on being a wife and mother. Believe that your past is making you better for your bright future ahead.

PRAYER FOR THE DAY: *Heavenly Father, thank you for keeping my mind together. Thank you today for your promises of a bright future ahead for me and my children. Be with us as we strive to not dwell in the past. Please give me strategies to move forward. Help me to use my past to help other. In your name I pray. Amen.*

Recommended Scriptures: *Jeremiah 29:11; Philippians 3:13; Ephesians 4:31; Galatians 2:20, Hebrews 12: 1-2 2 Corinthians 12: 9- 10*

Reflections for Today

Day 4

Don't Give Up!

Scripture: But as for you, be strong and do not give up, for your work will be rewarded. 2 Chronicles 15:7 (NIV)

HOW MANY TIMES have you asked yourself on this journey, "How much more can I take?" Seems like everything you're trying it's not working. While it is working for everybody else. Seems like it's too much coming at you all at one time. The support system that you have does not seem to be enough. You find yourself wishing that you can clone yourself to get it all done.

How many days do you spend trying to keep up with everything? Your career, your new dual role as parent, trying to socially interact so everyone would stop lecturing you to have fun and forget your ex- or soon-to-be ex-husband, rebranding your life and the list goes on. Then there are those days that you just want to sit in the middle of the floor and cry. But you have to stay strong.

I personally know that feeling of wanting to give up. I felt that I would never get my children back. I'd been fighting for over 5 years. I'd spent so much money on legal representation. I was living from paycheck to paycheck and the end of the custody battle seemed nowhere in sight. One night I pushed myself to go to a prayer meeting. With my journal in hand, I sat in the middle of the floor told God "I give up." I had no hope left. I'd made up my mind to just let my ex-husband get the kids. But God met me sitting in the middle of that floor. The Pastor who led the meeting began to speak to me and said "God said you cannot give up. You cannot give up on getting your children back." It's as if she had read my journal. I knew that was God speaking directly to me. She prayed with me as the other women surrounded me. I left from that meeting with renewed strength and hope.

Other times of wanting to give up came. But each time I focused not on the next day, but on getting through that next hour by hour reminding myself that God is holding my hand and holding me up.

Know that in your weakness and when you are ready to give up, God is always with you. He really does hear your cry and feel your pain. When you are weak He gives you strength. Even if that strength comes through him sending other people to help you.

God always lets you know that you are not alone. When you are at the end of your rope, tie a knot and hold on.

PRAYERS: *Dear Lord, today I feel like giving up. Please give me the strength to carry on continue believing that you are going to get me through this point in my life. You said in your Word that your grace is sufficient for me for your power is made perfect in my weakness. Today I am trusting you for making me strong at this time when I'm ready to give up.*

Recommended Scriptures: *Phil 4:13; 2 Corinthians 12:9; Isaiah 40: 29-31; Isaiah 41:10; Deuteronomy 31:6*

Reflection for Today

_____

_____

_____

_____

_____

_____

_____

_____

_____

_____

_____

_____

_____

_____

_____

_____

_____

_____

_____

_____

_____

_____

_____

_____

Day 5

Don't Panic!

Scripture: Do not be anxious about anything, but in every situation, by prayer and petition, with thanksgiving, present your requests to God. Philippians 4:6(NIV)

PANIC IS NOT JUST FEAR, but an uncontrollable fear, feeling of anxiety and being overwhelmed. You're already stressed and overwhelmed so panic over takes you so much easier. Especially when everything seems to be coming at you all at once; that feeling of having to keep so many balls in the air. This is a recipe for making wrong decisions.

If a truth be told, panic seem to be have become your companion from the moment you heard the word divorce. That feeling of anxiety the moment he told you, or you made the decision to get a divorce. That panic about being a single mother for the first time, or the first time in a long time. Now all of this on your own; take care of your children, pay all the bills alone, take care of a home all alone. It feels like learning to ride a bicycle for the first time. So many things that you're responsible for;

quick decisions to make.

What about coming home and the lights are off or the water has been turned off? And you don't have enough money in the bank to cover a reconnection fee. What do you do? So many balls that I had to keep in the air. Sometimes having the money but forgetting to pay that bill. Overwhelmed. Everybody was depending on me. Those eyes looking at me worried. I had to do some quick thinking. I hated asking anybody for help. I had to calm down and begin to pray; remember God's promises to me. Some days it was hard to do that. But I did it. And it worked. Even times when I did not have the money God granted me favor. I would always pray that the right person with the right heart would answer the phone.

When panic takes over, remember to stop and pray. Remember that God will never leave you.

PRAYERS FOR THE DAY: Be anxious for nothing. Today I will meditate on those words. I will trust you Lord to handle every situation for me. I have faith that everything will work out in my favor. Thank you for your peace. Amen.

Recommended Scriptures:: Philippians 4:7; Psalm 56:3; 2 Timothy 1:17; Joshua 1:9; Colossians 3:15

Reflections for Today

_____

_____

_____

_____

_____

_____

_____

_____

_____

_____

_____

_____

_____

_____

_____

_____

_____

_____

_____

_____

_____

_____

Body

Day 6

Self-Care: 911

Scripture: .....In repentance and rest is your
salvation, in quietness and trust is your strength,
but you would have none of it. Isaiah 30:15 (NIV)

AS I LAID BACK, MOUTH WIDE OPEN, dental tool
in my mouth, tears rolled down my face. This was a
pivotal moment for me. How did I let it get this far? Here
I was facing an extraction of a tooth that I'd already
spent so much money on with a previous root canal.
Then another procedure on the same tooth. Now
extraction of that tooth? All because I had not taken the
time to return to my dentist to complete the procedure.

Running, running. Taking care of children. The fight
with custody and divorce proceedings. Trying to put my
best foot forward at work, while also a graduate student.
Trying to make things work on one income.

I took no time for myself. No time for self-care. No down
time other than to pray. And prayer because it helped me
stay sane.

I laid there mad at myself. In trying to keep all the balls in the air, I'd dropped one; MYSELF. I was losing weight, not because I exercised, but because I was not eating. I took no time to reconnect socially. Work. Children. School. Ministry. This was my cue to take care of me. I hadn't put on my oxygen mask first, then everyone else's. As a result, I was breaking.

Self-care is important. Take time to refuel. Take time to retreat. Take time to pause. Find peace within yourself. Hear your voice. Hear God speak to you. Take time to smell the roses. Reconnect with self. Then connect on a deeper level with others. Exercise, even if it's only a few minutes a day. Read a book just for fun. Reconnect with hobbies you had put down after getting married and starting a family.

Make a commitment to take care of YOU. Think, if you don't take care of you, are you truly taking care of the others entrusted to you?

PRAYER: *Lord, thank you for making me aware of the need to take care of me. Thank you for reminding me that I need to take care of me. Reminding me that I matter. Please show me ways, starting today, that I can take better care of me; without excuses. Amen*

Recommended Scriptures: *Psalm 139:14; 1 Corinthians 6:19-20; 3 John 1:2; Ephesians 5:29-30; Exodus 33:14; Psalm 127:1-2*

Reflections for Today

Day 7

God Covers Your Shame

Scripture: Those who look to him are radiant; their faces are never covered with shame. Psalm 34:5 (NIV)

UNDER THE MICROSCOPE. That's the first thought that comes to mind at some point on this journey. You feel is of everybody is looking at you, people are judging you, people are talking about you. You feel as if you've been dissected and placed under microscope for people to peer into every single microscopic area of your life.

Lies are being told about you; parts of your life that should have remained private. Those are the parts that spouse and attorney, and even his family and friends seem to want everybody to know. The slander. The shame. Ashamed even when you know you shouldn't be. It's enough that everyone knows your home has been split. You're already feeling pain and the uncertainty of moving forward with your life. You just want to live in peace. You want to shelter your children.

I am a very private person. A person had to be in my inner circle to know what was going on. Imagine my shame when someone on my job at a university, told me she knew about the domestic abuse. I was even more embarrassed because he also worked there. She had met both of us when we were students at the same University. The look of pity on her face made me feel small. She apologized to me saying she knew that it wasn't my fault. I still wanted to go somewhere and hide.

A few months later, people started telling me everywhere I went that I looked different; that I was glowing. Then I discovered today's scripture. I found some peace in these words.

Yes, God's radiance really does cover your shame. Stand on this promise. Each time you feel ashamed reach back to today's scripture. God is protecting you and covering you. He will never allow you to be brought to shame. Even in your mess God will cover you.

PRAYER FOR THE DAY: *Lord, I stand on your promise today to cover my shame. Please strengthen me to keep my head held high in the midst of this journey. Thank you for walking with me. Amen.*

Recommended Scriptures: *Isaiah 61:7; Pssalm 25: 2 -3; Psalm 25:20; Psalm 31:17; Psalm 31:1; Psalm 35:4*

Reflections for Today

_____

_____

_____

_____

_____

_____

_____

_____

_____

_____

_____

_____

_____

_____

_____

_____

_____

_____

_____

_____

_____

_____

Putting the Pieces Back Together

Scripture: God, pick up the pieces. Put me back together again. You are my praise!
Jeremiah 17:14 (MSG)

A STORM CAME INTO YOUR LIFE. It's a storm named Divorce. Scattering the pieces of your life in many different places. Your family, your mind, your spirit and your possessions. Everything around you fell apart. You felt broken on the inside. You're left in a place to figure out how you are going to put the pieces of your life back together again. You may have asked "How am I going to survive this? I can't even think straight."

To start a new journey of putting the pieces of your life back together, you must first be honest about where you are. Examine every area of your life. But at the same time don't drop your broken pieces. Hold on to them. Don't throw them away.

See the beauty of the new you. God is smoothing out the rough places where you were mended back together.

Even with all you've endured and experienced, God is wanting to use you to make a difference in the lives of others.

Think of these women in the Bible and how he used their brokenness. Esther was an orphan and faced the challenge of saving her people, but she married a king. Ruth and Naomi both lost their husband, but God gave made them both a part of a family again.

As you put the pieces of your life back together, focus on your strengths. The pieces will be fused together just right. Your strengths will be the glue.

PRAYER FOR THE DAY: *God thank you for helping me to maintain my sanity as I pick up the pieces of my life. Thank you for helping me to keep my children's minds and lives together. Be with us as every area of our lives are mended. Amen.*

Recommended Scripture: *Leviticus 6:21; Acts 27: 27 – 24; 1 Peter 5:10; Psalm 71: 20 – 21; Joshua 1:8, Matthew 11:28; John 10:10*

Reflections for Today

_____

_____

_____

_____

_____

_____

_____

_____

_____

_____

_____

_____

_____

_____

_____

_____

_____

_____

_____

_____

_____

_____

$\mathcal{D}ay$ 9

God Your Protector

Scripture: So we say with confidence, "The Lord is my helper; I will not be afraid. What can mere mortals do to me?" Hebrew 13:6 (NIV)

AT NIGHT –SECURITY CHECKS —doors locked; windows closed; exterior lights on; interior lights out; alarm on. Kids tucked in bed. Checking noises at night. All these tasks are now your responsibility. As a wife, this was not. You've been conditioned to depend on your husband for this. You felt that protection. You could step back, and let him deal with it. He covered you. At least, that's what you rested in.

Now you're at that place where you're in that fight for your life. In addition, you have to protect your reputation, your physical space, as well as you and your children's peace of mind.

After being married for twelve years, and no longer accustomed to living alone, I worried about someone breaking into the house at night or even while we were away. Eventually, I became OCD about checking doors while we were at home. Insomnia became my friend. I was terrified at the realization that I was now my children's first defense. I'd have to be the adult to face an intruder. What if they got to my kids first? What would I do? At this point, I'd experienced having lived through domestic violence in my marriage, his love for guns, his anger, and the things they were saying about me caused me to live in fear of something happening to me. Sad, but he's the one I called when I heard a noise outside my window one night. We're so used to that husband being there that he's the first one we think of when it comes to impending danger near the home. Even though, he may have been the one that caused us harm and distress too.

At some point, God began to ask how much did I depend on Him as God at the time during marriage? Did I make Him secondary? Did I trust God to protect us or did I leave that up to my husband?

Now, you are at that moment that you realize you need to intentionally depend on God to protect you and your children. God was there all along. Find peace within yourself.

Today, trust that God has you and your children protected. Trust that He will not let any harm come to you. Know that he will defend you, at home, at work, in the courtroom, and when confronted by those against you. God is with you and never leaves you.

PRAYER: FOR THE DAY *Today Lord, I trust you totally for the protection of me and my children. We will lie down in peace and sleep. Amen*

Recommended Scripture: *Isaiah 51: 7-8, 12; Psalm 91; Psalm 3:3; Isaiah 43:2; 2 Thess 3:3*

Reflection for Today

_____

_____

_____

_____

_____

_____

_____

_____

_____

_____

_____

_____

_____

_____

_____

_____

_____

_____

_____

_____

_____

_____

Day 10

Your Femininity

Scripture: You are altogether beautiful, my darling; there is no flaw in you. Song of Songs 4:7 (NIV)

MAKEUP...HIGH HEELS...FITTED DRESSES..... Pretty in pink.... Flirty smiles.... Being demure.... Where did those days go? When was the last time you even felt like a demure female or in the mood to dress up, and do all these things?

As a wife, mother, career woman, sister, leader and more, most women are so busy trying to do it all. We wear so many hats, and are expected to stay strong through it all. For the sake of not appearing weak, we don't want to look as if we are not capable of fighting for equality in various sectors of our lives. We learn not to show vulnerability. Even at home, we are often times not appreciated. Stressed. Overwhelmed. Depression becomes our companion that we secretly bask in. Unhappy, but with smiles on our faces. There is no more time, nor are we in the mood anymore for the girly stuff. We do just enough for it to seem as if we care.

We just gave up on having those times where our husband would open doors and pull out chairs. It seemed as if chivalry was dead. We got used to doing all this for ourselves. However, we didn't realize that we were burying the parts of us that God made us uniquely a woman. The parts that made us feel and act feminine. We were just existing as a woman, but with no femininity that we had to put any effort into. Again, there is no time for the girly stuff.

I went from tomboy to tennis girl, to beauty queen, to feeling frumpy, and not caring during marriage. This was my story. Most of my energy went into trying to keep my mind together, and fighting off depression and unhappiness. Smiling for the public. Trying to keep up the appearance of a happy wife and mother. A leader in church. Still, I felt dead inside, and didn't care about all that. I didn't like what I saw in the mirror. And for a long time, I did not have the mental nor spiritual energy to make a change. I'd gained over one hundred pounds between babies, stress, and not taking care of myself. Whenever I did muster up some strength to do it, to dress up sexy, to flirt with my husband, to do all the things I knew how, my husband most times did not appreciate it. So, I gave up completely.

You may now be in that place where you are asking yourself if you are still desirable. You may have felt this way during marriage. Now, you are discouraged about your femininity. You feel your energy is needed elsewhere. However, because God designed you to be female, this is a necessary part of your restoration process.

Webster dictionary defines femininity as the quality of being feminine; quality of being a woman. This tells us that being feminine is not just what we have on – makeup or clothes or shoes – it's what we feel on the inside of us that defines our femininity. Psalm 139:14 tells us that we are fearfully and wonderfully made. Therefore, God looks at us women from the inside out to be a woman. Balancing our confidence and independence along with our feminine side can happen.

It's time to uncover the feminine you that you lost. Begin to feel your beauty from the inside out. Take a look in the mirror today, and remind yourself that you are altogether beautiful; there is no flaw in you.

PRAYER FOR THE DAY: *Lord, please help me to not be ashamed to show that the feminine side of me exists. Please protect me as I find myself again. Guide me and give me wisdom I renew and rebuild from the inside out.*

Recommended Scriptures: *Proverbs 31:7; Psalm 139:14-16; 1 Peter 3: 3-4; Genesis 1:27*

Reflections for Today

_____

_____

_____

_____

_____

_____

_____

_____

_____

_____

_____

_____

_____

_____

_____

_____

_____

_____

_____

_____

_____

_____

Spirit

Day 11

Faith & Trust

Scripture: Trust in the Lord with all your heart and lean not on your own understanding Proverbs 3:5 (NIV)

FEAR AND FAITH SEEMS TO GO HAND-IN-HAND! We hardly ever see one without the other. The phrase 'have faith' is so easily thrown around but oftentimes we don't really think about what it takes to grasp the essence of what faith is; especially when we're at a place in our journey we hardly have time to think.

At this point in your life going through a divorce, or if your divorce is final, you probably have many moments where you are so afraid and unsure. This is a new place where you alone have to make decisions that can make or break not just you, but your children too. You are so afraid of what's going to happen next. Wondering if you're making right decisions.

For me, my main challenge was fear in regards to finances. I was worried about how I was going to make ends meet, how I would keep the lights on, how I would pay for my children's needs. Many days I didn't feel as if I had the mental and physical stamina to make it through all that involved the divorce proceedings and custody battle. While performing satisfactorily at work and being there for others too.

Many days I had to draw on all that I knew about the God in me. Something in me would not let me totally give up; at times coming down to the 11:59th hour. I had to trust Him to take care of all that concerned me and my children. Each time I trusted God, it always worked out for me.

It's not just a saying, but truth - in order to have faith you must trust in what you can't get see. So dig into yourself, and find that part of you that becomes vulnerable to trust and have faith in the one that created you.

PRAYER FOR THE DAY: God today I trust that you have me and my children in the palm of your hands. I trust that you will never leave us nor forsake us. You have not given up on me. You want the best for me. So I thank you for guiding me on this journey. Amen

Recommended Scriptures: Ephesians 3:16-17; Mark 11:24; Hebrews 11:1; 2 Corinthians 5:1; James 1:6

Reflections for Today

_____

_____

_____

_____

_____

_____

_____

_____

_____

_____

_____

_____

_____

_____

_____

_____

_____

_____

_____

_____

_____

_____

Day 12

Restoration: Mind, Body & Spirit

Scripture: Restore to me the joy of your salvation and grant me a willing spirit, to sustain me.
Psalm 51:12 (NIV)

TAKE A LONG LOOK IN THE MIRROR. Really see yourself. Your mind, your body, your spirit. Where did you go? Who is this woman that you are now? Do you see a version of your former self? Most of us on this journey are worn out, our minds are jumbled, our bodies are not cooperating because we hardly took time for ourselves and we are fighting to stay connected to our Creator. We are just existing, not truly living.

There is a fight within yourself to get YOU back. Get your mind focused. Get your body healthy. Get your spirit back feeling totally connected to God where you truly feel you are one of His again. You are ready for total restoration in your mind, body and your spirit. But where do you start?

Restoration starts with you making up your mind to heal and move forward and knowing because of God's promises that there is good ahead for you. It starts in the mind to get healthy in your body. And it starts in the mind to reconnect to the Lord of your life.

Through my own journey, I held fast to God's promises in his Word, that He would restore me. Throughout the divorce proceedings, and after it was final, throughout the custody battle for seven years, losing custody of my children for two years, the process of restoration continued.

Don't be so hard on yourself. Just start somewhere. Begin to fortify your mind and your spirit with God's promises for you. Believe His promise to restore you and each child.

PRAYER FOR THE DAY: *Dear God thank you for being patient with me as I go through this process. Please help me to be patient with myself. Amen*

Recommended Scriptures: *Joel 2: 25–26; Jeremiah 30:17; Isaiah 61:7; Job 42:10*

Reflections for Today

_____

_____

_____

_____

_____

_____

_____

_____

_____

_____

_____

_____

_____

_____

_____

_____

_____

_____

_____

_____

$$\mathscr{D}ay \ 13$$

That 'F' Word: Forgiveness

Scripture: Be kind and compassionate to one another, forgiving each other, just as in Christ God forgave you. Ephesians 4:32 (NIV)

FORGIVENESS....A DIRTY WORD in your vocabulary right now. It's hard to see beyond the pain, the anger and the regret of having invested time in a relationship that has ended. Perhaps, you're dealing with betrayal. You've put so much of your life into this relationship. You've been told and even been taught that you need to forgive because God forgave you. It's easily said, but not so easy to do right? Of everything that you need to do to move on, forgiving the man that you intended to spend the rest of your life with is usually the most difficult.

"What if I'm the one who ended the relationship?" you're saying? In this case, often you are having a hard time forgiving yourself or you still find yourself blaming him. In most cases divorced mothers ponder, "What could I have done differently?"

Many people feel that forgiveness means that you should trust the person again, be friends with him and be okay with what happened. That's not forgiveness. Forgiveness is letting go of the pain, the resentment, the feelings of betrayal so that you can move forward. Forgiveness is not allowing these negative feelings to hold you hostage, and feeling like a victim of your relationship with your ex-husband.

For me, I had an easier time forgiving my ex-husband for the physical, verbal and mental abuse than I did him taking my children away from me. Those were two long years only seeing my babies every other weekend during the school year. I had to fight off feelings of hating him. I didn't want to hear what God was saying to me about forgiveness. Nor, did I want to hear from others telling me that. They were not the ones experiencing what I did. I was mad at myself too for even making the choice to get married to him. Forgiving myself was hard. I had to work hard and allow God to heal my heart. I finally got to this point after my children was allowed to be with me at the end of two years. I saw that my not forgiving him was also hurting my children. It was hard work, but I did it. And it is still a work in progress.

Forgiving the other person(s) empowers you. First, by giving you a peace inside and allows you to be able to move forward with your life. Holding on the hurt and the pain distracts you from seeing and moving toward your bright future. I know it's hard. And right now, you are probably having a hard time even letting today's topic minister to you.

From experience, I can tell you that when you finally get to that point of forgiving yourself or forgiving him and others attached to the situation, you would have reached a huge milestone in your journey. Allow God to minister to your heart today as you meditate on the scriptures. Allow the Lord to move you one step closer to your healing. Be honest with yourself and with the Lord today. Begin that process. Forgive.

PRAYER FOR THE DAY: *Lord, you know that today this is a hard one. This is one of the most difficult things to do, but you instructed me in your Word that I must forgive as you've forgiven me. Help me to search my heart today for all unforgiveness. Not just my ex-husband and the father of my children, but anyone in my life that I need to forgive. Be with me as I walk this journey. Thank you for getting me past this juncture. Amen*

Recommended Scriptures: *Colossians 3:12 – 13; Matthew 18: 21 -22; Romans 12:19; Matthew 6:15; Luke 6:37*

Reflections for Today

_____

_____

_____

_____

_____

_____

_____

_____

_____

_____

_____

_____

_____

_____

_____

_____

_____

_____

_____

_____

_____

_____

_____

Day 14

Choose Your Battles

Scripture: He inquired of the Lord, saying, "Shall I go and attack these Philistines?   1 Samuel 23:2 (NIV)

FIGHTING TO STAY AWAKE, FIGHTING TO GO TO SLEEP, fighting to keep the smile on your face, fighting to keep your children together, fighting to keep the tears at bay, fighting during divorce proceedings. Everything seems to be a fight these days. Your whole life seems to be about fight and the need to win and not lose anymore. You feel as if you don't fight you'll lose everything that you've work so hard for. You've already lost him. So many people are telling you how to fight, when to fight, and even when you should give up. You're trying to make sure that you make the right decisions.

You're tired so you're not thinking straight to make decisions based on your faith. You feel as if God is not even fighting for you anymore. You do what comes naturally to you; you go into battle mode.

But should you fight every battle? I learned the hard way during my divorce and custody proceedings that I needed to choose my battles wisely. Some battles I had have faith and trust in God that He loved me enough to take care of them for me. I finally asked God for wisdom. I made moves only as God told me to make moves and the way He told me. It always worked. Even when it seemed like nothing was happening God was moving on my behalf

Choosing your battles wisely gives an opportunity for the other person's plans to be exposed, allows God to do his work and allows you to see God working for you as it strengthens your faith. You are able to then focus on moving forward. Not trying to fight every battle, or what seemed like a battle, gave me peace and a clear mind to take care of my children and getting us settled into our new way of life.

This day, get focused, talk to God about which battles you need to turn over to him.

PRAYER FOR THE DAY: *Lord this day please forgive me for not trusting you enough to fight my battles for me. Help me this day to turn everything over to you. I ask you for wisdom moving forward. Help me to use strategies that you give to me, even if it's through another person. Give me peace this day as I turn all this over to you. I trust you Lord. Amen.*

Recommended Scriptures: 2 Chron 20:17; Deut 20: 1-9

Reflections for Today

Day 15

Vertical Conversation: God Can You Hear Me?

Scripture: Therefore I tell you, whatever you ask for in prayer, believe that you have received it, and it will be yours.   Mark 11:24 (NIV)

GOD! CAN YOU HEAR ME! This was often my cry at the beginning and for years after my divorce proceedings. Most days, it seemed too much to bear. I felt so overwhelmed, and that I couldn't take anymore. The pain, carrying the load of being a "suddenly single" divorced mother was so much. Have you ever felt this way?

It seems as if you are doing all the right things – you've been praying, believing, even at times going on a fast. You're doing everything everyone else tells you to do. You've forgiven, or you are working on it. Yet, roadblocks seem to be in the way. You seem to be having a much harder time than he has. It appears that he is so easily moving forward with his life, while here you are struggling with your life. You are the one with the children and he's taking the easy street. For some of you, he's not even a person who prays. You were always the one that prayed in the family. So, why are things so hard for you?

The night I had to turn my children over to him to live with him almost two hours away, I asked God these same questions. I wondered why was I living my life in alignment with what I read in my Bible and knew to do? Why if he was the one who didn't care about all that, was he was allowed to take my babies away? I felt that God did not love me, so what was the use trying to live for Him? I wanted to rebel. Just go out there and live life on the edge. Even though this had never been my character. I wanted to stop praying because I felt God wasn't hearing me anyway. I felt so let down in that courtroom the day when the judge didn't even take time to hear my case; just made the decision to make me leave my babies with a man who had never been their main caregiver. I felt let down when no matter how much I worked or tried, no matter how much I tithed, my money still wasn't enough. Felt let down when my lights got turned off, or we didn't have heat in the house, or the water was turned off. And I had nobody to turn to. Or so I felt.

You may be like me. Despite feeling this way, that God is not hearing you, deep down something on the inside won't allow you to give up on God. Or rather, that God has not given up on you. Something in your spirit takes you back to the times when you know God did hear you. The times you cried out to Him to protect you while being abused, or to keep you from losing your mind during your marriage. God is the one that got you out of it alive. You and your children. Think back on your prayers then. Think of all the that you came through even before your marriage to this point.

God assures us that He does listen to us when we come to Him and pray. He was at work all along.

You may not understand in the beginning. But after a time as your faith increase, and you believe more in God even when it does not look like He is hearing you, you will know that He is there. Your answer may not come the way you want or at the time you would like, but God always gives us an answer.

PRAYER FOR THE DAY*: Lord, please forgive me for thinking that you do not hear me. Please teach me to hear your voice more as you speak to me. Continue to build my trust and faith in you. Be with me today as I exercise these characteristics. Amen.*

Recommended Scriptures*: 1 John 5:14; Job 22:27*

Reflections for Today

Finance

Day 16

God Is Your Source

Scripture: The Lord is my Shepherd, I lack nothing.
Psalm 23:1 (NIV)

GOD'S GRACE IS SUFFICIENT.....yes, we are on His mind. As I stood in the check out line at the grocery store one night four years ago, my card kept declining. I know I had money in that account, so I kept patiently insisting and the cashier kept trying. At the same time I was apologizing to this young white couple who stood next in line. Finally, a manager came over, tried and then told me that I'd have to use another form of payment. I told her, that all the money I had was on that account. I didn't get upset. I apologized again to the couple behind me again and started to walk away.

As the manager apologized again, I heard the cashier saying, "I'll have to ring all of it up again". Then he called out to me "He said he is going to pay for all your stuff". The young guy who stood behind me, said "Yes, I'm going to pay for your stuff. People have done it for my wife before, and my sister. So, I don't mind doing it for you." The items that I had taken off to see if maybe the card would go through with less, he told the cashier to add those back too. As I stood there, I heard the Lord saying to me "See I do love you. I do hear you. I do honor your trying to walk right with me in your singleness." I tried not to cry as I stood there. The wife refused to give me their name and number because she knew I would try to pay them back. Which was my exact reason for asking. She said no, no need to.

Then, as we both walked outside separately, we were shocked to realize that we had parked right in front of each other! Of all the cars in the parking lot, we were parked facing each other! Then he told me that they were going to go in the self-check out line, but changed their minds at the last minute and came in that long line behind me. I had done the same thing; changed my mind about the self-checkout and patiently waited.

For me this whole thing was even more profound, because around Christmas time, I had gone in this same store, card kept declining even with money there. That time too, someone paid for my items; the manger that came to assist. She told the cashier "Give me the stuff, I'll pay for them so she can take food home to her children and get to them.

There is a divorced mother reading this who does not know how you are going to make it from one day to the next, even financially. But trust that the Lord will take care of you and honor your walk with Him.

I have so many stories, just from one month alone; the Roadside Assistance company owner putting gas in my car and telling me to pay him at the end of the month and do that anytime I run out of money for gas; coming home to a manicured lawn because the young man who cuts my almost acre yard saying this one was on him because I couldn't afford it this time, the Pastor who took me to the gas station and put gas in my car. The female friends who gave me when I didn't have.

My sister, you don't have to compromise your integrity for things to be done for you. You don't have to give up your body to get resource. God is your source. Sometimes trusting is not easy, but as you take one day at a time, He will honor it. Even as most of my money for 5 years went towards lawyer fees to get my babies back, I still trusted the Lord. And as you do that, God will put the most unlikely people in your path to extend His arm.

PRAY FOR THE DAY: *Today, I thank you for where I am now. It could have been worst. Thank you for taking care of me and my children. Help me to trust you as you provide all of our needs.*

Recommended Scriptures: *Psalm 37; Psalm 115:14; Phi 4:19; Psalm 81:10; Matthew 6:33*

Reflections for Today

_____

_____

_____

_____

_____

_____

_____

_____

_____

_____

_____

_____

_____

_____

_____

_____

_____

_____

_____

_____

_____

_____

Day 17

Career: Now What?

Scripture: For I know the plans I have for you,"
declares the Lord, "plans to prosper you and not to
harm you, plans to give you hope and a future.
Jeremiah 29:11(NIV)

YOU HAVE A CAREER THAT was working for you
during your marriage. Now, that you are a one-parent
household, you are finding that your compensation
from this career is not adequate. Child-support may not
be enough. And to every other organization, you make
too much for assistance. But to you, it only looks good
on paper, never enough to cover the needs of you and
your children.

Or you may be a stay-at-home mom. You didn't have to
work. Your career was the Chief Operating Officer of
your home. A divorce caught you by surprise. You now
see the necessity to work. But what steps do you take
to get there? What career? It's been so long.
For many moms on this journey, some thought has gone
in to making a career change. This is a time of reflection
over your whole life. Your youth has flown past you
while you have invested most of your time in taking care
of and nurturing your family You may have made a few

changes, but always with them in mind.

This journey many times negatively affects your ability to perform like you used to at work; your organizational skills are suffering. Now a "suddenly single" mom, daily childcare is mainly your responsibility. Getting your children where they need to go and trying to get there to pick them up. There is not another parent to call on when you have to make the choice between picking up your child and staying late to meet that deadline at work.

Be mindful as you consider a new job, or totally changing career. You may be tempted to only consider the job because you have the potential to make a whole lot more money. Despite what society says, more money is not what defines success. More money may mean more time away from your children, and can also mean more stress.

For the first five years after my divorce and during the time my children came back home to me, I worked a job that on some days took me almost two hours to get home because of traffic. I stressed getting to my youngest to pick her up from afterschool. Many days, I would drive in to the school on two wheels. She'd be the last one for pickup. Those bright eyes look at me with tears if I was a few minutes late. I knew some changes in addition to the too little compensation had to be made.

Be prayerful as you make decisions about your career. Allow the Lord to guide you on this journey. Be careful to not desperately just take any job opening. And please don't accept or seek a position as proof to your ex-husband and others that you are indeed moving on with your life. Let your decision be based on what God shows you is a right one for your new family make-up. God does not want you to allow fear to shape your decision-making. This includes a decision about your career.

In the meantime, do your best where you are now. You never know what God has in store for you while you work your current position. Be sure that a career move is in alignment with God's will for your life.

PRAYER FOR THE DAY: *Lord thank you for your provision in this present time. Thank you that you have me on your mind. Please help me as I make decisions regarding my career. Help me to use wisdom. I want to move only as you tell me to move. In Jesus' name I pray. Amen.*

Recommended scriptures: *Ecclesiastes 5:10; Romans 12: 6-8; Ephesians 3:20 – 21; Proverbs 3:6; Matthew 16:26*

Reflections for Today

Day 18

Trusting God With Your Finances

Scripture: For where your treasure is, there your heart will be also. Matthew 6:21(NIV)

FINANCE IS UNFORTUNATELY ONE OF THE TRAUMAS of divorce. Nearly 2.8 million divorce takes place every year. Most divorce don't end amicably, especially in the area of finance. Assets have to be divided, decisions made about retirements, changes to beneficiaries and more. And then there are financials decisions regarding care of the child(ren) that you have together. Studies have shown that during the first year of divorce, the woman's standard of living is lowered while the man's standard of living increases.

You may be one of the "suddenly single" moms trying to make ends meet. Like I was, you are fighting to keep the same standard of living not only for you, but more importantly for your children. Where are you in trusting God with your finances? Especially if you were a wife who allowed your husband to handle that part of your lives. God wants you to trust Him with this area of your life too. God is not only concerned with your spiritual and physical well-being, but also your finances. God wants you to prosper.

To prosper, you must remain connected to God. God will give you strategies to stretch your money. God will give you favor to get extensions or decreases in debts owed. He will give you favor to have debt erase. But you need to trust Him to walk with you. I've experienced firsthand how God will give you favor to decrease the chaos in your finances. Trust in the one who gives you the health, strength and strategy to get the money.

PRAYER FOR THE DAY: *Lord thank you for the increase you have blessed us with. Help me to make right decisions where our finances are concerned. Help me as I trust you to guide me. I pray for wisdom. Amen.*

Recommended scriptures: *3 John 2; John 15: 4-5; Matthew 6:31–33; 1 Timothy 6:17; Galatians 3:29; Malachi 3:10*

Reflection for Today

_____

_____

_____

_____

_____

_____

_____

_____

_____

_____

_____

_____

_____

_____

_____

_____

_____

_____

_____

_____

_____

_____

_____

$\mathcal{D}ay$ *19*

Starting Over: Bare Minimum

Scripture: Taking the five loaves and the two fish and looking up to heaven, he gave thanks and broke the loaves. Then he gave them to his disciples to distribute to the people. He also divided the two fish among them all. They all ate and were satisfied, and the disciples picked up twelve basketfuls of broken pieces of bread and fish. Mark 6:41 – 43 (NIV)

I LEFT – with all of our clothes and a few pieces of furniture. I just wanted out. Had had enough of the abuse and the disrespect. I tried staying, praying that he would change his mind and go to counseling for anger management and then us as a couple. However, he was not hearing that. I'd had two near misses with strokes from the stress and the depression that I'd existed with for most of the twelve years while married.

At this point, most women don't care about the material stuff. We just want to get out alive and with our sanity intact, or what we had left of it. Some of us had to run with only the clothes on our backs and what we could fit into our vehicles for us and our children. We were trusting God to help us start over. You have no idea what the 'new' and the days ahead will bring, but you are trusting God that the new is better than the old.

Starting over, I didn't have much in the way of material possessions. But I had peace in my heart and my spirit. I felt a sense of renewed hope. I knew that God would replace the material possessions. Starting over increased my faith. The Lord reminded me to go back to the days before I got married. That resourceful and smart woman was still on the inside of me. As the Lord added to us, the more confidence I gained. Most of all, the more content I became.

On this journey, know that quality, not quantity is what is important. As the Lord shows you more about yourself, as God adds to you and to your home, your faith in God will increase. Know that God will take a little and make it much.

PRAYER FOR THE DAY: *Today Lord I thank you for giving me the courage to step out into my better. Please be with me and my children as you add to us. Amen.*

Recommended Scripture: Lamentations 3: 22-24; Psalm 40:3; Revelations 21:5; Luke 5:36-38

Reflection for Today

_____
_____
_____
_____
_____
_____
_____
_____
_____
_____
_____
_____
_____
_____
_____
_____
_____
_____
_____
_____
_____
_____
_____
_____

Day 20

You Are Not a Failure!

Scripture: My flesh and my heart may fail, but God is the strength of my heart and my portion forever. Psalm 73:26 (NIV)

ON THIS JOURNEY, the word failure has entered your mind several times. Failure as a wife. Failure as a mother. Failure to keep your word to yourself. You feel a failure for not being able to keep all the balls in the air. Some of them have dropped and caused a ripple effect. You may even feel like you've let down others because your marriage ended.

You've been hard on yourself. A perfectionist. You worry about what others are thinking about you. When was the last time you gave yourself a break? When was the last time you forgot about what everybody else wanted and began to say no? God does not expect you to be a perfect person. He wants you to lean on him.

Statistics show that divorce is number two on the Stressor Scale; only below losing a spouse to death. This places divorce one above the stress level of going to prison for life. Yes. Divorce is considered trauma. So the feeling of failure is normal. But still know that God is with you. His grace covers you and will be there to help you bounce back from any area of your life where you feel you have failed.

Many days after my separation and for years after my divorce, I beat myself up because I felt like I was a failure. Things didn't seem to be progressing like I wanted them to. This included on my job. I was used to being an overachiever. However, no matter how I tried I was having a hard time keeping up with my increasingly stressful responsibilities. I could never seem to be as organized and on top as I used to be. It never crossed my mind to take into account that I was dealing with the separation from my husband as well as the unexpected separation from my three children. I gave myself no slack; harder on myself than anyone else. It was difficult to focus. I had to really spend some time and talk to God. God showed me that I needed to stop trying to be so strong and lean on Him for strength and guidance. I say the same to you today. Reflect on ways you can begin to totally lean on your Creator. Remember, where there is life, there is hope.

PRAYER FOR TODAY: *Lord help me as I lean on you for strength and guidance. Help me to not stay down, but get back up and continue moving forward. In Jesus' name I pray. Amen.*

Recommended Scriptures: *2 Corinthians 12:9; Phil 4:13; 1 John 1:9; Prov 3: 5-6; Romans 3:23; Jeremiah 8:4*

Reflections for Today

Family

Day 21

Your Children:
Their Journey Too

Scripture: Train up a child in the way he should go: and when he is old, he will not depart from it.
Proverbs 22:6 (KJV)

AS A MOTHER, your children are your pride and joy. You know that a child is a gift from God. God knew them from they were in your womb; they were uniquely made. (Psalm 139:13-16) Most mothers try to stay in the marriage so that their children can be in a balanced home. You fought to keep the family together. Whether of your own actions or not, there are no longer two parents in the home. Now you are dealing with your own emotions as well as the emotional and physical well-being of each child. Unfortunately, this is their journey too.

They too are feeling grieved; not understanding why their parents cannot make it work. They sometimes try to fix things themselves. Feeling as if somehow it is their fault. As a mother you try to console; sometimes nothing helps. Sometimes, they blame you too. Especially if you are the parent that initiated the split. What can you do? Where do you turn?

If you are familiar with today's scripture, you know that the common meaning of this scripture is to discipline your children while they are young. We were taught that this scripture means to punish them.

However, we are also responsible for the way our children's minds are shaped. They are gifts to us from God and we are their caretakers here on this earth. We are to also train them up in the way family and relationship should positively function. Relationship in their home is their first lesson. When they see abuse or altercations in the home, are we training them up in the way they should behave and think? When they see negative behaviors they are also learning to carry on generational destructive behaviors. Do you as a mother want to train your child to be in an environment of abuse or consistent contention and then this is what they pass on as adults?

Because this is their journey too, know that this is also their time to grow in hearing and knowing God. Ensure that you teach them to pray and to ask God the questions that you have no answers for. They will in turn encourage you and be praying too for the future.

PRAYER FOR THE DAY: *Father, thank you for keeping the minds of my children. Be with them on this journey. Give them answers when I can't. Help them to trust you too. Amen.*

Recommended Scriptures: *Psalm 8:2; Matthew 21: 15 – 16; Psalm 127: 3 -4; Mark 10: 13-16; Jeremiah 1: 5-7*

Reflection for Today

_____

_____

_____

_____

_____

_____

_____

_____

_____

_____

_____

_____

_____

_____

_____

_____

_____

_____

_____

_____

_____

Day 22

Confidence As a Mother

Scripture: This is what the Sovereign Lord, the Holy One of Israel, says: "In repentance and rest is your salvation, in quietness and trust is your strength, but you would have none of it. Isaiah 30:15 NIV

TIRED is the most frequent word that pops in your mind. You are exhausted; physically, emotionally, mentally and spiritually. You wonder how you are making it from day to day taking care of yourself and those that depend on you. You get home from work and work begins again, Now the children only have you to call on. No moment when they can go to their dad to ask questions or just tell about their day. You try so hard to listen to them attentively, but your mind is on to the next chore or task. You have every intention to have some quiet time with God on a daily basis, but you fall asleep trying to do it.

Many days you feel guilty as you can tell they really want your attention, but you hardly have the mental energy. This guilt begins to open the door to the feeling of incompetence as a mother. You are feeling as if you have somehow failed your children.

My sister, when was the last time you really rested? Peacefully? Rested your mind and your body? See when we are tired we cannot think and focus as we need to. The time with God is needed. You not resting is a direct result of trying to control every area of your life.

This Includes motherhood, but you cannot do that without hearing from God. To hear from God, you need to get quiet. You can rest and be confident in knowing that God is putting your life back together (Ps 4:8) and that your children will still rise and call you blessed. (Proverbs 31:28)

As you become focused, God will show you more ways that you can connect with your children. Let them know that God is filling the gap for their father not being there on a daily basis. As you become more confident, they'll become more confident.

PRAYER FOR THE DAY: *Dear Lord, thank you for the gift of being a mother. Help me to raise each child according to your wisdom. Increase my faith as a mother. Thank you for entrusting me with them. Amen.*

Recommended Scriptures: *Mark 6:31; Matthew 11:28-30; James 1:17; Proverbs 17:6; Philippians 4:6-7*

Reflections for Today

Day 23

While The Children Are Away

Scripture: This is what the LORD says: "Restrain your voice from weeping and your eyes from tears, for your work will be rewarded," declares the LORD. "They will return from the land of the enemy. So there is hope for your descendants," declares the LORD. "Your children will return to their own land. Jeremiah 31: 16 - 17

ONE OF YOUR GREATEST CONCERNS as a divorced mother is what will happen when your child is away from you. Who are they allowed to be around? What are they being taught? Are they being treated right?

Many mothers are the main caregivers. We don't trust that the fathers are capable of doing all that's needed to be done for his child. There are very few men who was involved in all areas of their child's life. As a mother you walk that tightrope of protecting your children while trying to not make them feel as if they are a pawn on this journey.

For the first seven years after the separation, I had to fight for custody of my children. I was afraid that at anytime, the current custody arrangement could change and my babies would be taken away from me. That day came four years into it. For two years I didn't sleep at night. I was so worried about my children. We'd never been away from each other more than a weekend or a week in their entire lives. It was hard on us. One morning I woke up really depressed, but I reach for my Bible. My Bible shockingly opened to today's scripture. I'd never seen this before as much as I read my Bible. But the promise of the scripture, gave me hope. From that point on, through the court proceedings for two years, I held on to God's promises.

As we trust God to protect our children, God is also looking out for us as a mother. He will not let any harm come to your children. Know that while they are away from you, God is still taking care of them. Put your hope in this.

PRAYER FOR THE DAY: *Lord thank you for protecting my children while they are away from me. Teach their father to be a true protector while they are in his care. Please give me peace while they are away from me. Amen.*

Recommended Scriptures: *Isaiah 54:13; Proverbs 3: 5-6*

Reflection for Today

Day 24

Children: The Balance

Scripture: For I am the Lord your God who takes hold of your right hand and says to you, Do not fear; I will help you.   Isaiah 41:13 (NIV)

YOUR LIFE AS A MOTHER has been a balancing act. But it is even more challenging now. No one to throw the ball to. You have to figure it all out how to keep the balls in the air for you and your children.

Not only is physical balance necessary, but spiritual and emotional balance. You hurt, but you know that each child hurts too. What do you do as a mother to help them through this?

As the flight attendant tells us on an airplane, put on your own oxygen mask first before you help anybody else. Oxygen is needed for the brain to function at its best. In this case your oxygen is your connection with God. Your oxygen gives you life. You being alive and focused paves the way for you to help your children with school, with extracurricular activities, with social activities and ensuring family time in order to create a new normalcy for them.

God will give you the wisdom as you seek him to balance your life as well as the lives of your children. He'll give you wisdom on which activities to prioritize. He'll give you wisdom which activities you can eliminate.

PRAYER FOR THE DAY*: Lord thank you for helping me not to give up as a mother. Thank you for the gift of being a mother. I ask you today to please give me strategies to balance our lives and reduce stress and create peace in our homes. In your name I ask these things. Amen.*

Recommended Scriptures: *Phil 4:11, 13; Ecc 3:1 -8; Hebrews 13:5; 1 Peter 5:7; James 5:30*

Reflections for Today

_____

_____

_____

_____

_____

_____

_____

_____

_____

_____

_____

_____

_____

_____

_____

_____

_____

_____

_____

_____

_____

_____

_____

_____

Day 25

Letting Go!

Scripture: Get rid of all bitterness, rage and anger, brawling and slander, along with every form of malice. Be kind and compassionate to one another, forgiving each other, just as in Christ God forgave you. Ephesians 4: 31 – 32 (NIV)

LETTING GO can be one of the hardest things to do! Letting go of that relationship; letting go of being able to say 'my husband'; letting go of what has been your family for so long; letting go of the familiarity of what your life has been for many years. It's not easy. Letting go means stepping into an unknown future for you and for your children.

Even letting go of the pain, the fear, the resentment, the hurt, the anger, the hurtful words is a challenge. In the beginning it feels as if you will have to pretend it never happened. But letting go allows God to take control. Letting go of the past means that you are ready to face the future.

As you allow God to lead you, you'll realize that He wants to use your past to pave the way for you in your future. Trust God to hold your hand and lead you through this journey. Holding on to the baggage of the pain, trying to hold onto him in your mind, holding on to your idea of what family is, weighs you down. Holding on to all the mental and emotional baggage also brings on stress and stress-related sicknesses. Some of which you may be experiencing right now.

Give all of this to God and allow Him to show you new norms. Allow your experiences to open new doors for you. As reminded in Romans 8:28, you know that because you love the Lord, all things will work together for your good; even the bad experiences. Let the past move you into your future.

Letting go of the relationship in your heart will take time. And as you trust God through this period, you'll see that you've made room in your present and your future for a new and healthy relationship. Let go first for yourself. God promises that the plans he has for you are to prosper you and not to harm you. (Jeremiah 29:11)

PRAYER FOR THE DAY: *Today is another hard one Lord. But I trust you to let go of all that I should. Help me to move forward. Help me to release the baggage. I trust you. Amen.*

Recommended Scriptures: *Phil 4:11, 13; Ecc 3:1 -8; Hebrews 13:5; 1 Peter 5:7; James 5:30*

Reflections for Today

_____

_____

_____

_____

_____

_____

_____

_____

_____

_____

_____

_____

_____

_____

_____

_____

_____

_____

_____

_____

_____

_____

Relationship

Day 26

Friendship: Revised

Scripture: A friend loves at all times, and a brother is born for a time of adversity. Proverbs 17:17 (NIV)

FAIR WEATHER FRIEND. Ever heard that term? Those friends that are there only during the good times. When challenges come to you, they are nowhere to be found. Most divorced mothers expect to lose some friendships. But we expect those to be the people that we met as a result of our ex-husband. It's shocking when girlfriends who were your friend before your marriage disappear and are not there to support you. It's like you've become a disease.

You call, and they never answer. Nor do they return the call. You're already feeling like you've lost everything. And now some friends that you expected to be there are no there anymore? And then there are those girlfriends who try to keep you away from their husbands. As if all of a sudden because you are no longer with yours, that you will try to take her husband away. This is furthest from your mind. You just want the support of your friends.

A true friend will be there for you through thick and thin. Even if she thinks you're wrong, she'll support you in public and then rebuke you in private. On this journey she'll be there with you even when everybody else listens to the slander. She'll find time for you even with her busy life. She will truly love you at all times.

I've experienced both ends of the spectrum. Friends sticking with me. And friends leaving me. One in particular that shocked me was a close friend from my church. She was like a big sister to me. A single mother. I supported all of her visions and dreams. To my surprise, when I asked her to help me move she told me "no", and that she didn't want my ex-husband to think badly of her. I was so hurt. She'd been through a divorce, so she could empathize but didn't. On the other hand, I had one friend, when I couldn't sleep at night, stayed up with me until I got sleepy; usually around three or four a.m. And we both had to get up early that morning to be at work.

Many days, especially on the weekends, my phone did not ring at all. God was revising my definition of friendship. No more fair-weather friends were allowed in my life.

Search your friendship database. And be honest with yourself as God is exposing and revealing those true to you. In this season of your life don't try to hold on to people that God is showing you are not going to be a true friend who sticks with you.

PRAYER FOR THE DAY: *Lord thank you for those friends that stuck with me through thick and thin. Help me to let go those who left me. Thank you for those that you are bringing to me in the future.*

Recommended Scriptures: *Prov18:24 & 16:28; John 15:13*

Reflections for Today

Day 27

Rebuilding Trust in Yourself

Scripture: I praise you because I am fearfully and wonderfully made; your works are wonderful, I know that full well. Psalm 139:14 (NIV)

THROUGH THIS JOURNEY, you've questioned and second-guessed yourself so many times. To the point that you don't believe nor trust your judgment anymore. You look at your choice of a husband, and begin to berate yourself as regret set in. You feel guilty for all the pain that your children have suffered. All because of your choice you think. You took the burden on yourself and wear it as a yoke around your neck.

You've questioned who you are as a woman, who you are as a mother, who you are in your career. You've even doubted that you are pleasing God in the way you walk with him. In the years during your marriage, you may have been told, as I was, that you are not a good lover, nor a good person. The way he criticized you chipped away at your confidence in who you are as a person. My ex-husband would tell me that nobody liked me. And that no other man would want me. I unconsciously began to believe that.

As I began to meditate and renew my relationship with God, he reminded me that I am fearfully and wonderfully made. Made in the image of God. (Psalm 139:14) Here's your reason to trust in yourself. God does not make junk. He took his time making you to fulfill a specific purpose in this earth. He formed you in your mother's womb. He didn't just throw some cells together. "Indeed, the very hairs of your head are all numbered. Don't be afraid; you are worth more than many sparrows." Luke 12:7 (NIV) Does that not let you know that God cares and loves you?

Trust in the God who took his time to make you. As you build trust in him and begin to move as God leads you, you'll begin to have more confidence in the person that he made; you. Make decisions according to what you've been taught by God. Always take His presence with you.

PRAYER FOR THE DAY*: Lord as I work on believing and trusting myself again, help me to trust you more. Help me to hear clearly from you. I ask in your name, Amen.*

Recommended Scriptures: *Prov 3: 5-6; Isaiah 41:10; Hebrews 11:1; Isaiah 43: 1-4; Luke 12:7*

Reflections for Today

_____

_____

_____

_____

_____

_____

_____

_____

_____

_____

_____

_____

_____

_____

_____

_____

_____

_____

_____

_____

_____

_____

Day 28

Spread Your Wings

Scripture: But those who hope in the Lord will renew their strength. They will soar on wings like eagles; they will run and not grow weary, they will walk and not be faint. Isaiah 40:31 (NIV)

For so long, you've lived to please and to be there for everyone else. Especially, the husband and the children. You continuously place yourself on the back burner. You hardly remember what it feels like to lift your wings and take flight. You may have fleeting thoughts of pursuing your dreams, but each time you try, someone else's dream or crisis became your priority.

You even have your Vision Board to prove that you intended to make some changes. For once, since becoming a mommy and wife, you were going to just do it. Do something where you can pursue your passion. Now with so many balls in the air; you're afraid again. Everyone tells you that you need to concentrate on getting your children through this.

God wants to lift you above all of your burdens and the things that you think are priority but above his purpose for you. He's waiting on you to spread your wings like an eagle to fly towards your purpose. Your purpose is just not for you. Your purpose is also for you to build legacy for your children. Your purpose is to reach back and help another woman through this journey.

If I'd never found the courage to spread my wings, despite my fatigue and fear, you would not be reading these words on this page. Spreading my wings allowed me to reach you in the pages of this Devotional that especially speaks to your journey. Listening to who God said I am. Trusting that He will catch me if I fall, allowed me to have the courage to spread my wings to encourage you. I spread my wings so that you can have hope and be reminded that God loves you and wants the best for you.

Verse 30 above today's scripture reference reminds us that even the young get weary and needs strength. So be encouraged that even though you are tired, God will give you the strength to keep going as you begin to spread your wings. As you spread your wings more, you'll become more confident in yourself and in your journey. IT's in spreading your wings where your purpose for this season in your life is discovered.

PRAYER FOR THE DAY: *I thank you today Lord for being the wind under my wings. Give me strength as I reach for my dreams and begin to live out your purpose for my life. I trust you Lord. Amen.*

Recommended Scriptures: *Prov 3:5-6*

Reflections for Today

_____

_____

_____

_____

_____

_____

_____

_____

_____

_____

_____

_____

_____

_____

_____

_____

_____

_____

_____

_____

_____

_____

_____

Day **29**

Break Your Silence!

Scripture: For Zion's sake I will not keep silent, for Jerusalem's sake I will not remain quiet, till her vindication shines out like the dawn, her salvation like a blazing torch. The nations will see your vindication, and all kings your glory; you will be called by a new name that the mouth of the Lord will bestow. Isaiah 62: 1-2 (NIV)

AS WOMEN, especially after we get married, we're taught to not speak about anything that happened in our homes. We don't speak about things that happened during our relationship. We are told to do this so that others cannot get in our business. And what if we tell the secrets and others end up not liking our spouse? We learn to be caged in secrecy. Many of us hold in the secrets of infidelity and abuse. And many times we feel like we are the only one dealing with it.

As I sat on the stand in the courtroom being questioned during my divorce proceedings, six of my friends sat in shock as I began to recount the instances of abuse. Even my best friend had not heard most of what I told that day. I'd hid it from everyone. From friends, and from family. I'd told a few things but predominantly wrote about them in my journal. I was for the first time breaking my silence. This gave him room to say that I lied. Because I didn't have a lot of proof. During the years that followed this court hearing, I began to talk of it a little more to women that I met who were experiencing the same things. Many told me how I'd helped to save their lives by my not being afraid any longer to speak my truth.

God has given me a mandate that I had to help other women become free. I could no longer think of being ashamed, but tell my story anyway. Was facing my shame and protecting my reputation more important than saving a life?

You'll find that breaking your silence not just frees another divorced mother, but it also frees you. Speaking about your experience when led by the Lord will also help to release you from your shame, your guilt and the pain that's associated with your experience. You'll begin to see purpose in the experience you endured.

As you step out and break your silence, you've experience for yourself, that all things do work together for the good of those who love the Lord and are the called according to His purpose. Don't wait – break your silence!!

PRAYER FOR THE DAY: *Lord please give me the courage to open my mouth and break my silence. I want to walk in obedience to your purpose for my life. Amen.*

Recommended Scriptures: *Prov 3:5-6*

Reflections for Today

_____

_____

_____

_____

_____

_____

_____

_____

_____

_____

_____

_____

_____

_____

_____

_____

_____

_____

_____

_____

_____

_____

Day 30

Loving Again

Scripture: And so we know and rely on the love God has for us. God is love. Whoever lives in love lives in God, and God in them. 1 John 4:6 (NIV)

DIVORCE IS the dirty "D" word that causes so much pain and suffering for almost everyone involved. Divorce brings shame and guilt. Infidelity may have been involved. There may have been domestic abuse in different forms. You and your children suffered. This causes most divorced moms to shy away from even thinking of the word LOVE again. Because love should protect not bring pain.

You are probably tired of everyone telling you when you should start looking for love again; or telling you to "just get out there". Statistics show that there is no specific right time period. Only you know the right time for you.

A word of caution – be sure that you've worked on loving yourself before you look to love someone else. Or before you look for someone to love you. Before moving on, are you confident in God's love for you? Do you believe that you are the apple of his eye? (Psalm 17:8) Do you believe that God loved the whole world, even you, so He gave His son to die for you? That kind of love? (John 3:16)

If you are confident in God's love for you, also know that He will protect your heart on this journey to being open to loving again. As a result of your past experiences you now have more wisdom when it comes to this part of your life. I learned more about love, when I allowed myself to truly bask in the love that God has for me. My revelation was that a man is just God's representative of showing a woman how He feels for us in the flesh.

Trust God to protect you as you embark on this journey again.

PRAYER FOR THE DAY*: Lord, I know firsthand how love can bring hurt instead of happiness. How it can expose and bring pain instead of protecting. I ask you today to please be with me as I open my mind and heart to love again. Protect my heart as you send the right one to find me. Amen.*

Recommended Scriptures: *Job 42:10; John 3:16; 1 John 4:18; Psalm 17:8*

Reflections for Today

_____

_____

_____

_____

_____

_____

_____

_____

_____

_____

_____

_____

_____

_____

_____

_____

_____

_____

_____

_____

_____

_____

_____

_____

_____

Breakthrough Moments

BREAKTHROUGH MOMENTS

Journal your ah-ha moments for the past 30
    days of using this Devotional

_____

_____

_____

_____

_____

_____

_____

_____

_____

_____

_____

_____

_____

_____

_____

_____

_____

_____

_____

_____

_____

_____

_____

_____

_____

_____

_____

_____

_____

_____

_____

_____

_____

_____

_____

_____

_____

_____

_____

About the Author

Darlene Hollis, a native of the Bahamas, is a divorced mother of three(3), a transformational speaker, an ordained minister, servant leader, certified Life Coach and so much more. Many wouldn't think that something so tenacious and profound could come from the heart and drive of someone who is quiet and shy. Darlene is full of compassion for women all across the world; equipping them to embrace their inner beauty as it so beautifully shows up on the outside. Darlene is passionate about the things that affect women daily, self-worth. Her resilience is found in the way she has bounced back and broken her own silence. Darlene speaks confidently and authoritative to every environment that she is placed in. Ministry starts with you first and Darlene knows firsthand.

There came a time in Darlene's life where what she faced, many would have lost it. Darlene encountered her own "Fork in the Road" experience. She was going through a divorce after 13 years of marriage and then lost custody of her 3 jewels (children) for 2 years. Here you had a scientist and she could not find a cure for her own brokenness; a midwife who needed someone to help her push through; a former University Administrator and she needed someone to help organize, strategize and make sense of the chaos that was currently happening in her own life. Singing, prayer, praise and determination got Darlene to the place of restoration with her children and to the point of gaining enough strength to break her silence about what she had experienced.

Known as 'The Confidence & Personal Resuscitation Coach' (The CPR Coach), Darlene became the vehicle in which God would use to birth, coach and restore girls and women, local and abroad. Being the trailblazer that she is "Broken Silence Ministries, "Am I really my Sister's Keeper" Women's Conference and "Who Am I?" Teen Girls Conference were birthed. Women and girls all over are compelled to share their stories to overcome shame and to let other women know that there is still hope and that you must speak up for what you want and believe in; the silence must be broken.

If this Devotional has helped you to get some breakthroughs, please leave a review.

You can sign up for the email list and special bonuses at bit.ly/dmdevotional

Follow me on Facebook and Instagram at Darlene Hollis – The CPR Coach

Periscope : @BrokenSilenceGA

Thanks for reading! I pray this Devotional made a difference in your life. Please add a short review on Amazon and let me know what you thought!

Subscribe to my email list at bit.ly/dmdevotional and receive a free bonus download offer for Divorced Moms.

DH Books International

For information contact :
DH Books International
289 Jonesboro Road
Suite 145
McDonough, GA 30253

Web: bit.ly/dmdevotional
Email : dhbooksinternational@gmail.com

ISBN: 978-1981154630

88506945R00071

Made in the USA
Columbia, SC
06 February 2018